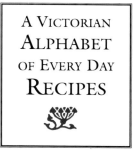

A Victorian
Alphabet
of Every Day
Recipes

WE MAY LIVE WITHOUT
POETRY, MUSIC AND ART,
WE MAY LIVE WITHOUT CONSCIENCE
AND LIVE WITHOUT HEART;
WE MAY LIVE WITHOUT FRIENDS;
WE MAY LIVE WITHOUT BOOKS,
BUT CIVILIZED MAN CANNOT
LIVE WITHOUT COOKS.

FROM LUCILE, 1860,
BY OWEN MEREDITH 1831–1891

A VICTORIAN
ALPHABET OF EVERY DAY RECIPES

26 ORIGINAL RECIPES
FROM MRS. ISABELLA BEETON
TAKEN FROM HER BOOK OF
COOKERY AND HOUSEHOLD MANAGEMENT

A BULFINCH PRESS BOOK
LITTLE, BROWN AND COMPANY
BOSTON • NEW YORK • TORONTO • LONDON

Copyright © 1993 by Inklink

Illustrations by Robin Harris

First North American Edition

First published in Great Britain in 1993 by
PAVILION BOOKS LIMITED

Library of Congress Cataloging-in-Publication Data
Beeton, Mrs. (Isabella Mary), 1836–1865
A Victorian alphabet of every day recipes / Isabella Beeton –
1st U.S. ed.
p. cm.

ISBN 0-8212-2034-9
1. Cookery, English. I. Title
TX717. B483 1993
641.5941 – dc20   92 – 44026

BULFINCH PRESS IS AN IMPRINT AND TRADEMARK OF
LITTLE, BROWN AND COMPANY (INC.)
PUBLISHED SIMULTANEOUSLY IN CANADA BY
LITTLE, BROWN & COMPANY (CANADA) LIMITED.

PRINTED IN HONG KONG

Alphabetic Table of Contents

THE
SCIENCE OF COOKERY

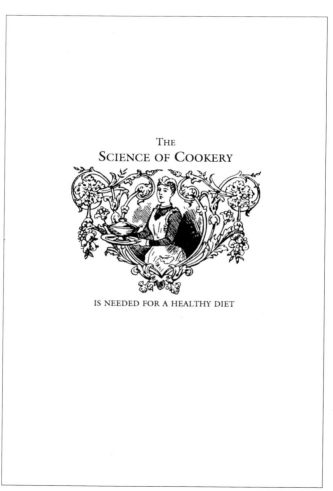

IS NEEDED FOR A HEALTHY DIET

PREFACE

N THE DAYS BEFORE refrigerators, freezers and supermarkets, planning and provisioning a balanced menu for the average household was very much a day-by-day affair. The choice of foods presented at table was limited to seasonal and local availability, and yet Victorian cooks went about the task of preparing appetizing family meals with thrift, tenacity and imagination as this delightful selection of twenty-six recipes admirably demonstrates. We hope you enjoy this opportunity to sample once again mouth-watering dishes from over one hundred years ago when fresh ingredients and good home cooking were the order of the day.

BON APPETIT!

PPLE JELLY ——————
THICK, OR MARMALADE
(for Entremets or Dessert Dishes).
INGREDIENTS *About 2 lbs. apples, 1¼ lbs. sugar cubes, lemon-peel.*

PEEL, CORE, AND BOIL the apples with only sufficient water to prevent them from burning; beat them to a pulp, and to every 1 lb. (2 cups) of pulp allow ¾ lb. of sugar cubes. Dip the cubes into water; put these into a saucepan and boil till the syrup is thick and can be well skimmed; then add this syrup to the apple pulp, with sufficient grated lemon-peel to flavour the jelly, and stir it over a quick fire for about 20 minutes, or till the apples cease to stick to the bottom of the pan. The Jelly is then done, and may be poured in moulds which have been previously dipped in water, when it will turn out nicely. A little custard may be poured round, or it may be stuck with blanched almonds.

TIME.–*From ½ to ¾ hour to reduce the apples to a pulp; 20 minutes to boil after the sugar is added.*
SEASONABLE; *at any time.*

APPLE JELLY, STUCK WITH ALMONDS.

IX

BEEF,
ROAST SIRLOIN OF.– INGREDIENTS
10 – 16 lbs. beef, a little salt.

AS A JOINT cannot be well roasted without a good fire, see that it is well made up about ¾ hour before it is required, so that when the joint is put down, it is clear and bright. Choose a nice sirloin, the weight of which should not exceed 16 lbs., as the outside would be too much done, whilst the inside would not be done enough. Split it or hook it onto the jack firmly, dredge it slightly with flour, and place it near the fire at first. Then draw it to a distance, and keep continually basting until the meat is done. Dish the meat, sprinkle a small quantity of salt over it, empty the dripping pan of all the dripping, pour in some boiling water, stir it about, and strain over the meat. Garnish with tufts of horseradish, and send horseradish sauce and Yorkshire pudding to table with it.

The rump, round and other pieces of beef are roasted in the same manner, allowing for solid joints rather more than ¼ hour to every lb.

TIME.– *A Sirloin of 10 lbs., 2½ hours; 12 lbs., 14 to 16 lbs., about 4 or 4½ hours.*
SEASONABLE; *at any time.*

OD'S HEAD
AND SHOULDERS ————————

INGREDIENTS *A nice fresh cod's head & shoulders. Sufficient water to cover the fish; [5 oz. of salt to each gallon].*

CLEANSE THE FISH thoroughly, and rub a little salt over the thick part and inside of the fish 1 or 2 hours before dressing it, as this very much improves the flavour. Lay it in the fish-kettle, with sufficient cold water to cover it.

Be very particular not to pour the water on the fish, as it is liable to break it; and only keep the water just simmering. If the water should boil away, add a little by pouring it in at the side of the kettle, and not on the fish. Add salt in the above proportion, and bring the water gradually to a boil. Skim very carefully, draw it to the side of the fire, and let it gently simmer till done. Take it out and drain it; serve on a hot napkin, and garnish with cut lemon and parsley.

TIME.– *According to size, ½ an hour more or less.*
SEASONABLE; *at any time.*

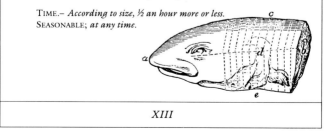

AMSON PLUM CHEESE ───────

INGREDIENTS *1½ pints (2 cups) of damsons to each pot.– Damsons; to every lb. of fruit pulp allow ½ lb. of sugar cubes.*

PICK THE DAMSON STEMS, and put them into a preserving-pan; simmer them over the fire until they are soft, occasionally stirring them; then beat them through a coarse sieve (strainer), and put the pulp and juice into the preserving pan, with sugar in the above proportions, having previously carefully weighed them. Stir the sugar well in and simmer the damsons slowly for 2 hours. Skim well, then boil the preserve quickly for ½ hour, or until it looks firm and hard in the spoon; put it quickly into shallow pots, or very tiny earthenware moulds, and when cold, cover it, with waxed papers, and the jars with tissue-paper brushed over on both sides with the white of an egg. A few of the stones (pits) may be cracked, and the kernels boiled with the damsons, which very much improves the flavour of the cheese.

TIME.– *1 hour to boil the damsons without the sugar; 2 hours to simmer them slowly ½ hour quickly.*
SEASONABLE; *Make this May through to September.*

GGS, SCOTCH

INGREDIENTS *for dish for 4 persons.–*
6 eggs, 6 tablespoonfuls of forcemeat,
made with anchovies or ham for
flavouring, hot lard, ½ pint of good
brown gravy.

BOIL THE EGGS for 10 minutes, strip them from the shells, and cover them with forcemeat. Fry a nice brown in boiling lard, drain them before the fire from their greasy moisture, dish them, and pour round them a ¼ to ½ pint of good brown gravy. To enhance the appearance of the eggs, they may be rolled in beaten egg and sprinkled with bread-crumbs: but this is scarcely necessary if they are carefully fried. The flavour of the ham or the anchovy in the forcemeat must preponderate, as it should be very relishing.

TIME.– *10 minutes to boil the eggs, 5 to 7 minutes to fry them.*
SEASONABLE; *at any time.*

OWLS, Simmered With Oysters

(Excellent). Ingredients *for dish for 4 to 6 persons.– 1 stewing hen about 5 lbs., 2½ dozen oysters, the yolks of 2 eggs, ¼ pint (⅔ cup) of cream.*

Truss a fowl as for boiling; fill the inside with oysters which have been bearded and washed in their own liquor; secure the ends of the fowl, wrap it in foil securely, and plunge it in a large saucepan (stewpan) filled with boiling water. Keep it simmering for 1½ hours, or rather longer; then take the gravy that has flowed from the oysters and fowl, of which there will be a good quantity; stir in the cream and yolks of the eggs, add a few oysters scalded in their liquor; let the sauce get quite *hot*, but do not allow it to *boil*; pour some of it over the fowl, and the remainder send to table in a tureen. A pinch of ground mace added to the sauce, with the cream and eggs, will be found an improvement.

Time.– *1½ hours.*
Seasonable; *at any time.*

Oysters.

XIX

GOOSE, HASHED

(Cold, Meat Cookery.)
INGREDIENTS *The remains of cold roast goose, 2 onions, 2 oz. (4 table-spoonfuls) of butter, 1 pint (2½ cups) of boiling water, 1 dessertspoonful of flour, pepper and salt to taste, 1 tablespoon of port wine, 2 tablespoon-fuls of mushroom ketchup.*

CUT UP THE GOOSE into pieces of the size required; the inferior joints, trimmings, &c., put into a stewpan to make the gravy; slice and fry the onions in the butter of a very pale brown; add these to the trimmings, and pour over about a pint (2½ cups) of boiling water; stew these gently for ¾ hour, then skim and strain the liquor. Thicken it with flour, and flavour with the port wine and mushroom ketchup in the above proportion; add a seasoning of pepper and salt, and put in the pieces of goose; let these get thoroughly hot through, but do not allow them to boil, and serve with sippets of toasted bread.

TIME.– *Altogether, rather more than 1 hour.*
SEASONABLE; *from September to March.*

ARE JUGGED

(Very good.) – INGREDIENTS *for dish sufficient for 4 or 5 persons. – 1 hare, weighing about 3¾ lbs., 1½ lbs. of beef gravy, ½ lb. (1 cup) of butter, 1 onion, 1 lemon, 6 cloves; pepper, cayenne and salt to taste: ¼ pint (⅔ cup) of port wine, red-currant jelly.*

SKIN, DRESS AND WASH THE HARE, cut it into pieces, dredge them in flour, and fry in boiling butter. Have ready 1½ pints (3¾ cups) of gravy made from the above proportion of beef, and thickened with a little flour. Put this into a large thick piece of foil; add the pieces of fried hare, an onion stuck with 6 cloves, a lemon peeled and cut in half, and a good seasoning of pepper, cayenne and salt; wrap the foil down tightly, put it up to the neck into a deep stewpan or Dutch oven of boiling water, and let it stew until the hare is quite tender, taking care to keep the water simmering. When nearly done, pour in the wine, and add a few forcemeat balls; which have been fried or baked in the oven for a few minutes. Serve with red-currant jelly.

TIME.– *3½ to 4 hours. If the hare is very old allow 4½ hours.*
SEASONABLE; *from September to the end of January.*

CED-PUDDING

INGREDIENTS *½ lb. of sweet almonds, 2 oz. of bitter ones, ¾ lb. of sugar, 8 eggs, 1½ pints (3¾ cups) of milk, a few slices of citron or preserved cherries. Flavour with either vanilla curaçao or maraschino.*

BLANCH AND DRY THE ALMONDS thoroughly in a cloth, then pound them in a mortar until reduced to a smooth paste; add to these the eggs, well beaten, the sugar and milk; stir these ingredients over the fire until they thicken, but do not allow them to boil; then strain and put the mixture into the freezing-pot; surround it with ice and freeze it. When quite frozen, fill an iced-pudding mould, put on the lid and keep the pudding in ice until required for table; then turn it out on the dish. This pudding may be flavoured with vanilla, curaçao or maraschino liqueur.

TIME.–*½ hour to freeze the mixture.*
SEASONABLE; *Served all the year round.*

ICED-PUDDING MOULD.

ELLIES, Bottled

How to mould.– Bottled jellies, of which some of the best we think are sold by the firms of Crosse and Blackwell, and Goodall, Backhouse and Co., are very convenient and easily prepared desserts.

To mould them, uncork the bottle; place it in the top of a double saucepan over boiling water until the jelly is reduced to a liquid state; taste it to ascertain whether it is sufficiently flavoured, and if not, add a little wine. Pour the jelly into moulds which have been soaked in water; let it set and turn it out by placing the mould in hot water for a minute; then wipe the outside, put a dish on the top and turn it over quickly. The jelly should then slip easily away from the mould and be quite firm. It may be garnished as taste dictates.

OPEN MOULD.

KIDNEYS, Broiled

(A Breakfast or Supper Dish).

INGREDIENTS *2 sheep kidneys for each person, pepper and salt to taste, a little butter.*

ASCERTAIN THAT THE KIDNEYS are fresh and cut them open, very evenly, lengthwise, down to the root, for should one half be thicker than the other, one would be underdone whilst the other would be dried, but do not separate them; skin them and pass a skewer under the white part of each half to keep them flat and broil over a nice clear fire, placing the inside downwards; turn them when done enough on one side and cook them on the other. Remove the skewers, place the kidneys on a very hot dish, season with pepper and salt and put a tiny piece of butter in the middle of each; put them on buttered toast, serve very hot and quickly and send very hot plates to table.

TIME.– *6 to 8 minutes.*
SEASONABLE; *at any time.*

KIDNEYS.

OBSTERS, To Boil

INGREDIENTS *Lobsters, ¼ lb. of salt to each gallon of boiling water.*

BUY THE LOBSTERS ALIVE and choose those that are heavy and full of motion, which is an indication of the freshness. When the shell is incrusted, it is a sign they are old: medium-sized lobsters are the best. Have ready a stewpan of boiling water, salted in the above proportion; put in the lobster head downward and keep it boiling quickly, according to its size as given below and do not forget to skim well. If it boils too long, the meat becomes thready and if not done enough, the spawn is not red: this must be obviated by great attention. Rub the shell over with a little butter or sweet oil, then wipe this off again.

TIME.– *Small lobsters up to 1 lb. for 10 minutes, medium sized lobsters for about 15 minutes, lobsters about 2½ lbs. for up to 25 minutes.*
SEASONABLE; *all the year, but best from March to October.*

To Choose Boiled Lobsters This shell fish, if it has been cooked alive, as it ought to have been, will have a stiffness in the tail, which, if gently raised, will return with a spring. Care, however, must be taken in thus proving it; for if the tail is pulled straight out it will not return.

ACKEREL, Baked

INGREDIENTS *for a dish for 8 persons.– 4 mackerel, about 2lbs. each, a nice delicate forcemeat of 4 generous tablespoonfuls each, a little flour, 3 oz. (6 tablespoonfuls) of butter; pepper and salt to taste.*

CLEAN THE FISH, TAKE OUT THE ROES and fill up with forcemeat and sew up the slit. Flour and put them in a baking dish, heads and tails alternately, with the roes; and between each layer put some little pieces of butter and pepper and salt. Bake for ½ an hour in a medium oven at 350° degrees. and either serve with plain melted butter or a maître d'hôtel sauce.

IN CHOOSING THIS FISH, purchasers should, to a great extent, be regulated by the brightness of its appearance. If it has a transparent, silvery hue, the flesh is good; but if it be red about the head, it is stale.

MACKEREL.

TIME.– *½ hour*
SEASONABLE; *at any time.*

Note.– Baked mackerel may be dressed in the same way as baked herrings and may also be stewed in wine.

NECTARINES, PRESERVED ————
INGREDIENTS *to every lb.(2¼ cups) of sugar allow ¼ pint (⅔ cup) of water, 8 nectarines.*

DIVIDE THE NECTARINES IN TWO, take out the stones (pits), and make a strong syrup with sugar and water in the above proportion to cover all the nectarines. Put in the nectarines, and boil them until they have thoroughly imbibed the sugar. Keep the fruit as whole as possible, and turn it carefully into a pan. The next day boil it again for a few minutes, take out the nectarines, put them into jars, boil the syrup quickly for 5 minutes, pour it over the fruit, and, when cold, cover the preserve down. The syrup and preserve must be carefully skimmed, or it will not be clear.

TIME.– *10 minutes to boil the sugar and water; 20 minutes to boil the fruit the first time, 10 minutes the second time; 5 minutes to boil the syrup.*
SEASONABLE; *in June until August.*

Boiling Pot.

RANGE FRITTERS

INGREDIENTS *for dish for 6 persons.–*
For the batter, ½ lb. (2 cups) of flour,
½ oz. (1 tablespoonful) of butter,
½ saltspoonful of salt, 2 eggs, milk,
3 oranges, boiling-hot lard or
clarified dripping.

MAKE A NICE LIGHT BATTER with the above proportion of flour, butter, salt, eggs and sufficient milk to
make it the proper consistency; peel the oranges,
remove as much of the white skin as possible, and
divide each orange into eight pieces without breaking
the thin skin, unless it be to remove the pips (pits); dip
each piece or orange in the batter. Have ready a pan of
boiling lard or clarified dripping; drop in the oranges
and fry them a delicate brown from 8 to 10 minutes.
When done, lay them on a piece of blotting-paper
before the fire, to drain away the greasy moisture, and
dish them on a platter; sprinkle over them plenty of
pounded sugar, and serve quickly.

TIME.– *8 to 10 minutes to fry the fritters; 5 minutes to drain them.*
SEASONABLE; *at any time.*

HEASANT, ROAST ———————

INGREDIENTS *1 pheasant, weighing 2 to 3 lbs. flour, butter.*

OLD PHEASANTS MAY BE KNOWN by the length and sharpness of their spurs; in young ones they are short and blunt. The cock bird is generally reckoned the best, except when the hen is with egg. They should hang some time before they are dressed as, if they are cooked fresh, the flesh will be exceedingly dry and tasteless. After the bird is plucked and drawn, wipe the inside with a damp cloth, and truss it in the same manner as partridge. Roast it before a brisk fire, keep it well basted, and flour and froth it nicely. Serve with brown gravy, a little of which should be poured round the bird, and a tureen of bread sauce. 2 or 3 of the pheasant's best tail feathers are usually stuck in the tail as an ornament.

TIME.– *½ to 1 hour, according to the size until the juices run pink.*
SEASONABLE; *from September to the end of January.*

ROAST PHEASANT.

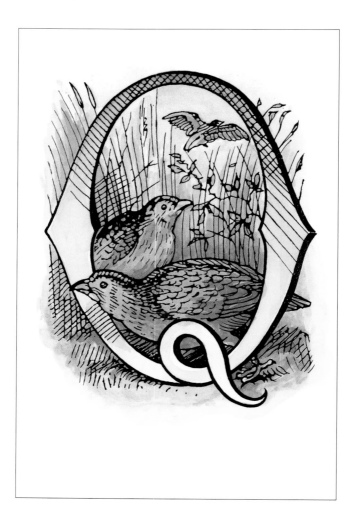

UAILS, To Dress

INGREDIENTS *Quails, butter, toast.*

THESE BIRDS KEEP GOOD for several days, and should be roasted without drawing, as the trails are, by epicures, considered a very great delicacy. Truss them in the same manner as woodcock; roast them before a clear fire, keep them well basted, and serve on toast.

THE QUAIL.

TIME.– *About 20 minutes.*
SEASONABLE; *from September through to January.*

QUAILS, CARVING OF. - *Quails being trussed and served like a woodcock, may be similarly carved, by cutting them exactly into two through the centre of their breasts.*

ABBIT PIE

INGREDIENTS *for medium-sized pie.–*
1 rabbit weighing about 3 lbs., a few
slices of ham, salt and white pepper to
taste, 2 pinches ground mace/or to
taste, ½ teaspoonful of grated nut-
meg, a few forcemeat balls, 2 hard-
boiled eggs, ½ pint (1¼ cups) of
gravy, about 1 lb. puff pastry dough.

CUT UP THE RABBIT, remove the breast-bone and
bone the legs. Put the rabbit, ham, forcemeat balls and
eggs, by turns, in layers, and season each layer with
pepper, salt, ground mace and grated nutmeg. Pour in
about ½ pint (1¼ cups) of water, cover with pastry
dough, and bake in a well-heated oven about 375
degrees., for about 1½ hours. Should the crust acquire
too much colour, place a piece of paper over it to prevent it from burning. When done, pour in at the top,
by means of the hole in the middle of the crust, a little
good gravy, which may be made of the breast and leg
bone of the rabbit and 2 or 3 lbs., shank-bones,
flavoured with onion, herbs and spices.

TIME.– *1½ hours.*
SEASONABLE; *from September to February.*
Note.– The liver of the rabbit may be boiled, ground and mixed
with the forcemeat balls, when the flavour is liked.

ALMON, Collared ———

INGREDIENTS *A piece of Salmon, say 3 lbs., a high seasoning of salt, ground mace and pepper; water and vinegar, 3 bay-leaves.*

SPLIT THE FISH; scale, bone and wash it thoroughly clean; wipe it and rub in the seasoning inside and out; roll it up and bind firmly; lay it in a fish kettle, cover it with vinegar and water (⅓ vinegar, in proportion to the water); add the bay-leaves and a good seasoning of salt and whole pepper, and simmer till done. Do not remove the lid. Serve with melted butter or anchovy sauce. For preserving the collared fish, boil up the liquor in which it was cooked, and add a little more vinegar. Pour over when cold.

TIME.– *⅓ hour, or rather more.*
SEASONABLE; *at any time.*

Salmon.

TURKEY, BAKED

(Italian Method Recipe)

INGREDIENTS *for dish for 8 persons.–*
A medium sized turkey weighing
about 8 lbs. ¼ lb. of sausage, 8 French
prunes, 4 pears, ½ pint (1¼ cups) of
boiled and peeled chestnuts, a glass of
Marsala or sherry, butter, salt, a few
slices of bacon and a little rosemary.

BLANCH AND CUT THE SAUSAGE into thin long pieces, blanch and stone (pit) the prunes, peel and quarter the pears; fry them with the chestnuts in a little butter for a minute or two; chop the liver of the turkey fine, and add it, then mix with the wine and make a forcemeat. Salt the inside of the turkey slightly and stuff with the forcemeat, and put it in the pan with the bacon, some butter, rosemary and a little salt. Place in a slow oven at 325 degrees., basting occasionally, till of a good colour. Serve with its own gravy.

TIME.– *About 2 hours.*
SEASONABLE; *all the year but best in November and December.*

ROAST TURKEY.

GLI- FRUIT PURÉE

INGREDIENTS *for generous servings for 4 persons you will need 2 ugli fruits, the juice of 1 freshly squeezed lemon, and a few drops of Maraschino liqueur.*

WASH THE UGLIS and cut in two. Then remove the pulp entirely and transfer this to a convenient nearby container, [retain the skins intact]. Add the Maraschino to taste and squeeze the lemon over the pulp. Gently blend the lemon juice and Maraschino into the pulp. You may now put the pulp into suitable dessert glasses or return it to the skins. Ugli-fruit purée is best served chilled.

For those of you unacquainted with this exotic fruit, an ugli fruit is a hybrid cross between a grapefruit and a tangerine. It resembles a small grapefruit with a warty skin which is brownish in colour. The orange coloured flesh within is quite delicious, and is described as tasting of peaches and melons. Uglis are grown in the West Indian Colonies.

SEASONABLE; *at any time. but being an exotic imported fruit, uglis are greatly subject to availability and price fluctuation.*
TIME.– *about 5 to 10 minutes.*

ENISON, STEWED

INGREDIENTS *for dish for 8 or 10 persons.– A shoulder of venison weighing 4 to 5 lbs., a few slices of mutton fat, 2 glasses of port wine, pepper and allspice to taste. 1½ pints (3¾ cups) of weak stock or gravy, ½ teaspoonful of whole pepper, ½ teaspoonful of whole allspice, red-currant jelly.*

HANG THE VENISON TILL TENDER; take out the bone, flatten the meat with a rolling-pin, and place over it a few slices of mutton fat, which have been previously soaked for 2 or 3 hours in port wine; sprinkle these with a little allspice and pepper, roll the meat up, and bind and tie it securely. Put it into a large stewpan or Dutch oven with the bone and the above proportion of weak stock or gravy, whole allspice, black pepper and port wine; cover the lid down closely, and simmer very gently from 3½ to 4 hours. When quite tender, take off the string, and dish the meat; strain the gravy over it, and serve with red-currant jelly. Unless the joint is very fat, the above is the best mode of cooking it.

TIME.– *3½ to 4 hours.*
SEASONABLE; *Buck venison and doe venison from September to the end of January.*

HITEBAIT, To Dress

INGREDIENTS *for dish for 3 or 4 per-sons.– 1–1¼ lb. Whitebait, a little flour, hot lard, seasoning of salt.*

THESE TINY SALTWATER FISH, such as herring, anchovy and smelt should be put into iced water as soon as bought, unless they are cooked immediately. Drain them from the water in a colander, and have ready a nice clean dry cloth, over which put 2 good handfuls of flour. Toss in the whitebait, shake them lightly in the cloth, and put them in a wicker sieve (strainer) to take away the superfluous flour. Throw them into a pan of boiling lard, very few at a time, and let them fry till of a whitey-brown colour. Directly they are done, they must be taken out and laid before the fire for a minute or two on a sieve (strainer) reversed, covered with blotting paper to absorb the fat. Dish them on a hot napkin, arrange the fish very high in the centre, and sprinkle a little salt over the whole.

TIME.–*3 minutes.*
SEASONABLE; *at any time.*

WHITEBAIT.

MAS PLUM PUDDING

INGREDIENTS *1½ lbs. of raisins, ½ lb. of currants, ½ lb. of mixed peel, ¾ lb. of fine bread-crumbs, ¾ lb. of ground suet, 8 eggs, 1 wineglassful of brandy, 1 lb. of sugar.*

CUT THE RAISINS IN HALVES, but do not chop them; wash, pick and dry the currants, cut the candied peel into thin slices. Mix all the dry ingredients well together with the sugar; moisten with the eggs, which should be beaten, and the brandy; stir well, and *press* the pudding into a buttered mould, tie it down tightly with a floured cloth, and boil for 5 or 6 hours. As the puddings are usually made a few days before Christmas, hang it up immediately. The day it is to be eaten, plunge it into boiling water, and keep it boiling for at least 2 hours; then turn it out of the mould, and serve with brandy-sauce. On Christmas day a sprig of holly is usually placed in the middle and about a wineglassful of brandy poured round it, which, at the moment of serving, is lighted, and the pudding thus brought to table encircled in flame.

TIME.– *5 or 6 hours the first time of boiling;*
2 hours the day it is to be served.
SEASONABLE; *on the 25th of December.*

YORKSHIRE PUDDING

(To Serve with Roast Sirloin of Beef.) – INGREDIENTS *for pudding for 6 persons.– 1½ pints (3¾ cups) of milk, 6 large tablespoonfuls of flour, 3 eggs, 1 saltspoonful of salt.*

PUT THE FLOUR INTO A BOWL with the salt, and stir gradually to this enough milk to make it into a stiff batter. When this is perfectly smooth, and all the lumps are well rubbed down, add the remainder of the milk and the eggs, which should be well beaten. Beat the mixture for a few minutes and pour it into a shallow tin (pan), which has been previously well rubbed with beef dripping. Put the pudding into the oven, and bake it for an hour; then, for another ½ hour place it under the meat, to catch a little of the gravy that flows from it. Cut the pudding into small square pieces, put them on a hot dish, and serve. If the meat is baked, the pudding may be placed under it, after the meat has been cooked some time and the dripping has been poured off, resting the meat on a small three-cornered stand.

TIME.– *1½ hours.*
SEASONABLE; *at any time.*

ZUPPA INGLESE

(English Trifle) INGREDIENTS *for a large dish. For the whip, 1 pint (2½ cups) of cream, 3 oz. (½ cup) of sugar, the white of 2 eggs, a small glass of sherry. For the trifle, 1 pint (2½ cups) of custard sauce, 6 slices of sponge-cake, 12 macaroons, 2 dozen ratafias, 2 oz. of sweet almonds, the grated peel of 1 lemon, a layer of raspberry jam, ½ pint (1¼ cups) of sherry, 6 tablespoonfuls of brandy.*

THE WHIP TO LAY OVER THE TOP of the trifle should be made the day before it is required for table, as the flavour is better. Put into a large bowl the sugar, the whites of the eggs, which should be beaten to a stiff froth, a glass of sherry and the cream. Whisk these ingredients well in a cool place, and take off the froth with a skimmer as fast as it rises, and put it on a sieve (strainer) to drain; continue whisking till there is sufficient of the whip, which must be put away in a cool place to drain. The next day, place the sponge-cakes, macaroons and ratafias in layers in a dish; pour over them sherry mixed with the brandy, and, should this proportion of wine not be found quite sufficient,

CONTINUED OVER

[ZUPPA INGLESE, CONTINUED]

add a little more, as the cakes should be well soaked. Over the cakes put the grated lemon-peel, the sweet almonds, blanched and cut into strips, and a layer of raspberry or strawberry jam. Pour the custard over the cakes, &c. The whip being made the day previously, and the trifle prepared, there remains nothing to do now but to heap the whip lightly over the top.

SEASONABLE; *at any time.*

TRIFLE.

A PLACE WELL LAID

A well-laid cloth enhances a well-made meal but there is more art than people imagine in laying a cloth properly.

Anyone can put a table-cloth over a table and add the necessary forks, knives, spoons &c., but everyone cannot place these things neatly and accurately, cannot think of everything that will be required, nor dispose either silver dishes or other adjuncts to look pretty and tasteful.

A well-laid table is one of the refining influences that home should bring to bear upon the young mind. Order, perfect cleanliness and good taste should be thought of as being essential at the table as in dress. Always have your table properly laid, and if it be done so every day, how much less the anxiety when guests are bidden to your table.

In a house where only one general servant can be kept, it may be that she has not always the time to lay the cloth. Rather than let this be done in a slovenly hasty way, it is better to do it oneself. There is nothing hard nor derogatory in this task; nay, it would be more so to sit down to a meal where everything was put on the table with neither thought nor care except that of getting the table laid in as short a time as possible.

You will require adequate sufficiency of the following chinaware items; Dinner Plates, Dessert Plates, Soup Plates, Side Plates & 2 Vegetable Dishes & 2 Salt Cellars, plus 1 each of, Soup Turine, Jug, Cheese Dish, Ice Pail,. Strawberry Dish, Spoon Warmer, Fruit dish.

You will require adequate sufficiency of the following chinaware items; Breakfast Cups, Bread & Butter Plates, Tea Cups, Coffee Cups and one each of, Tea Pot, Butter Dish, Bacon Dish, Bread Dish, Milk Jug, Sugar Bowl & Marmalade Jar.

A Victorian Alphabet of Every Day Recipes
was inspired by the work of
Mrs Isabella Mary Beeton (1836–1865),
British writer and author
of the most famous English cookery book,
The Book of Household Management (1861),
to whom we are indebted.
The work of Isabella Mary Beeton was first published
in the *Englishwoman's Domestic Magazine* founded by
her husband Samuel Orchart Beeton in 1852.
And subsequently published in volume form in many
and varied editions throughout the world.
The producers of this book also gratefully acknowledge
the many nameless artists and engravers who were
responsible for skilfully embellishing magazines & books
in the days before photography, and on whose work the
redrawn and newly coloured alphabet
illustrations are based.

Thank you